That Dude and His MOs

by Zsanece Brown and Consetta Brown

Illustrated by Ryan Smith

Digital Art by Ian Smith

That Dude and His MOs

by Zsanece Brown and Consetta Brown

Copyright © 2025 **Library of Congress**

All rights reserved.

Cover design and photography

by **Essentially Creative**

Illustrated by **Ryan Smith**

Digital Art by **Ian Smith**

Editing by **Writ Publishing LLC**

Baltimore, Maryland, United States

No parts of this publication may be reproduced, stored in a retrieval system, or transmitted in any form or by any means, electronic, mechanical, photocopying, recording, or otherwise, without the prior written permission of Zsanece Brown, except for brief passages quoted by a reviewer.

Under no circumstances may any part of this publication be copied for resale. To perform any of the above is an infringement of copyright law.

ISBN 979-8-9874739-1-7

Also by Zsanece Brown

Poetry

Of Wishes and Dreams
by Kale Rogers and Zsanece Smith
(Limited direct sale copies available)

defiance
by Zsanece Brown

distill'd – audio
Indigo – audio
Thank You – audio
Tousled – audio
f*** repression – audio
Taking Shallow Breaths Whilst Drowning – audio

Defiance – audio

by Essentially Zsanece

(Available wherever you download music)

Sketch Story

A Shadow's Depth – audio

by Essentially Zsanece

(Available wherever you download music)

Prose

Embracing Shadow: The Birth of Silent Dream

by Essentially Zsanece

(Available wherever you download music)

A letter to my son,

You hold so much promise, more than I'd ever hoped to be near. And I think that you've misunderstood your value at times. Weight from that can feel heavier than what you're ready for. But your value has never been attached to others' expectations. Those expectations, regardless of their claims, are reflections of how they see themselves.

Understand that how you see the world, despite how it too often sees you, is a rarity that we need right now. Keep assuming the best of others first, while letting yourself recognize and feel the energy that's at a person's core. Respond to what you know, be it an embracing of such or a protective stance and extension of what I consistently have in place over you.

You are invaluable. You're the very best of me. You are loved.

~Mom

~ Table of Contents ~

MOs - Definition 15

Preface 17

In His Own Words 18
Subtle Perfection 23
Oh no, Mos! 24
I am 25
Reflecting on an untitled piece 26
Heist 27
A quiet tempest 30
Untitled 31
Untitled 32
A "beautiful way of seeing and being" 33
Hypersensitivity 35
Open the Blinds 38

That Dude	40
Why quotes for diagnosed?	42
A slowly exhaled breath	45
Spontaneous Language	47
Expressive Language	49
Modeling Language	51
I'm fine	52
Adapting with Technology	54
Non-verbal Communication	56
Virtual Learning	58
Community-based Instruction	60
Cookies Are Life	62
MOs are master negotiators	63
MOs are also partners in crime	64
My mom, (also known as) Ma	67
What will that dude and his MOs do next?	69
Special Thanks	73
About the Authors	75

MOs • /mōs/

noun, plural

an overwhelming group of plush characters often including, but not limited to, several Elmos

"

Origin

<mark>Elmo</mark>, but plural

~ Preface ~

Hey, 4 a.m. It's me again. Ry and I have been up for about an hour now. He's pacing, but my mom calls it dancing. And I'm pretty sure she's onto something because, with the pacing, there's also humming and giggles. He discovered Tchaikovsky at about four years old. And I think that, this morning, he's experiencing one of his jams.

Sometimes, I have a good 30 minutes of indescribable silence before this – his joy. It's when I stir a little and reach for my phone to check the time. It's usually 3:33 a.m. and I'll think, *of course it is*. Silence isn't heavy at this time. Not at all. Instead, it's a slowly exhaled breath.

When you have a newborn, you're told to sleep when they sleep. But what if yours rarely slept, seemingly refreshed after quietly relaxing instead of napping? Maybe they also wake with giggles throughout the night. What if those newborn-months then stretched for 18 years? That's when 3:33 a.m. presents meaningful pauses.

In His Own Words

Ma found a small pile of folded-up papers hidden in the corner. The living room is small, but comfortable. The chocolate brown couch is low and soft. There's a metallic gold throw tossed on the end of the couch that has a chaise lounge.

Ian is the oldest and he likes to call the chaise lounge "his spot." The patio window's blinds are usually slanted just enough to let a little bit of light in. More warmth sneaks in than light, actually. Across from Ian's spot is our mini library. The books on the shelf that's eye-level start with the ones with red covers, then orange, then yellow, green, blue, and violet. The top shelf has all the books with the black covers and the third shelf has all the books with the white covers.

Mixed in are a few copper knick-knacks and a burnished-copper carousel music box that plays "Here Comes the Clowns." A squat and comfy caramel-colored chair sits at an angle and in front of the lower half of the bookcase. Behind that chair, on an unclaimed section of pale beige carpet, is one of Ryan's favorite hiding places.

The papers are folded, but bulky, since Ryan is still learning how to line up the edges before running his finger along the fold to give the page a hard crease. A few of the pages are just balled up loosely. As long as it's compact, he'll add it to his collection of papers.

I show him the folded-up pages in my hands and a couple of them fall to the floor because there are so many.

I shake my head and I tell him, "Not yours."

He frowns a little. *Want... not yours.*

"Some of these are important. Ok?"

Be back. He glances at the folded-up pages one more time before leaving the room.

~ * ~

A new book! It feels smooth. Bright reds. Dark blues, light blues. Big letters. Small numbers. Next page. Next page, (sniff)... Nice smell. Next page. Next page. Toys! One's a tablet. Tablets have games. Ian has games. And a phone. Phones play videos. I want Toy Story videos. Daddy has a tablet at his house. Ian plays with it. Mommy's laptop is for school. It has videos too, though. The password is all dots. Count them. One. Two. Three. Four.

Ryan gathers up his collection of papers and sits in Ian's spot. Ian glances with a raised eyebrow, but he decides to wait Ryan out to reclaim his spot. Ryan picks up a new Avon brochure from a stack, goes right to the middle of the brochure, and tears a page clean out of it.

"No, Ryan! Not yours," Ian tells him right away.

Want... not yours.

Peeking her head out of the kitchen and into the living room, Ma gasps.

"On no, Ryan! Those are mommy's new books, and she needs to give them away. No tearing pages. Ok? Not yours."

Be back. Ryan smoothed out the creases and glanced at it before tucking his treasure away on the side of the chaise lounge.

~ * ~

One of the times he pulled it out to look at it, Ma saw what was on the page. It was a picture of a tablet that was made specifically for young children and it was preset with educational games, songs, and videos. Ryan's autism affects how he sees the world and how he processes instructions. He doesn't have his own tablet and only plays with others' tablets, laptops, or phones with supervision.

Ryan was content, though, with carrying around this torn page that had just a picture of a tablet he wanted. Everyone around him was so intent on correcting him that we nearly missed out on seeing his world and understanding his words.

Subtle Perfection

The beauty in different approaches could be one of us...
looking for subtle shifts in color –
noticing how
when two blend, each softens.

And time slows...
enough to marvel at the focus of
one of us
who sees connections – lifting sections,
stacking parts of a whole.

Thinking in motion.
Moving through color.
Subtle perfection.

Oh no, MOs!

When I still lived with my parents and when my nephews were babies, my mom cared for them during the workday. And I absolutely rushed home after work to spend time with them. My oldest nephew assigned me the role of every female human lead character in whatever Disney or Pixar movie we watched. I've been Jasmine, Jane, and Mulan. I sang my songs and he knew his lines.

My mom collected plush characters and figures for his favorite movies. She would pull out a clear bin full of them for him to play with as he watched *Toy Story*, *Lion King*, or *A Bug's Life*. There was also a collection of *Sesame Street* plushies that easily had more versions of Elmo than any other character. This may be the origin story of MOs.

Years later and when my mom babysat my oldest son, I adored putting him in this super soft red romper. She took a picture of him once surrounded by all the Elmos she'd collected and sent it to me with the caption, "Oh no, MOs!"

I am

I am...

a force

awakened

enveloping the broken

lifting bent limbs

I am flowing...

Nourishing,

strengthening our roots

I am hidden,

nestled in her womb

Reflecting on an untitled piece

The second poem I wrote was about a dream. Little faces I couldn't see. We were alone, but I was certain that I heard their laughter.

I felt my boys long before I held them. I saw our path before their birth... I knew their likeness before I met them, saw the pastel shades of our life. Somehow, I knew.

And I was certain that I would be loved.

Heist

The first piece of art that I stole
was a line of poetry.
I walked around it slowly
as if it was a sculpture,
taking in the fullness of thought
of a four-year-old.

He told me that if rain was a color,
it would be gray.
And somehow his words complemented a day
that was both bright
and overcast.

I didn't ask if this verse,
in all of its completeness, was for sale.
Instead, I traced its edges with my fingertips,

hoping that the color of smoke

would stain them.

Removing his poetry from its gilded frame, I

rolled it up so that I could carry it with me.

He has a younger brother

and he has an artist's mind too.

In the spirit of Vermeer, peering

long enough to draw my attention to a tree, he

showed me that the darkness of its bark

was layered... textured.

Like Michael Angelo

seeing an angel in the marble

before carving to set him free, we

ignored the urge to touch

what may have been rough,

yet honest.

Pausing until I knew that the softness

and slightly uncomfortable feeling of moss

should be written in green ink.

I saw poetry

imbedded in an unlined page.

So, I wrote

until I set the moss free.

I stole my young one's way of seeing things,

removed it from its frame,

rolled it up

so that I could carry it with me.

A quiet tempest

I called my oldest son, my original cuddle bug, a "teenager-in-training" from the time that he was 10 years old until he was an actual teen. He's my techy, gamer, occasional sous chef. He's the person who changed me forever.

My firstborn is a very private person and I respect when he'd rather not have things about him shared. He remains my hope, dreams, and future. I'd be a different person without him.

I was blessed to be chosen to be this amazing being's mom. Those intense, dark eyes could sometimes be a quiet tempest... even in a car seat. An old soul, singing along with Smokey Robinson and the Miracles before he could even talk, explaining the emotions of the weather, assigning them colors. A poet already... at four years old.

Untitled

When the water evaporates,

it turns into a cloud...

A few days later, a little snowflake

heads towards the ground.

Then the wind blows it away.

The snowflake

ventures around a forest,

the sky,

and grasslands,

and it keeps going.

Then... the wind stops.

The little snowflake

falls on a pile of snow.

And two hours later...

the wind blows the snowflake

into the ocean.

- Ian, 10 years old

Untitled

The flower grows fast.

The bee goes crazy outside.

Spring is here again.

- Ian, 10 years old

*A "beautiful way of seeing and being" –
Kimberly*

One of my sisters-in-spirit mentioned that my explanations about how Ry may be experiencing the world seem to also be a general yet beautiful way of seeing and being in the world. I loved that and I want to share some connections I've made in the past related to this point because I honestly believe this to be true.

I believe that those who see the world differently are able to see what we may be missing. Bear with me. I'm about to wave my geek flag.

One of my favorite passages in something I read years ago was about Johannes Vermeer, who is believed to have used optics in his painting techniques. In the story, he asked his assistant what color the clouds were. She said white. He told her to look closer. She began to notice that the clouds actually reflected varied colors due to the atmosphere, sunlight, and so on. She noticed touches of blue, yellow, and gray along with the white. That fascinated me and I started to look for the layers of colors in everything around me.

I noticed Ry's precision very early on. He would be in a walker and he'd aim blocks or random tiny toys at a small opening some distance away from him. And they'd go in... every time. He's got an incredibly steady hand. I realized then, and I continue to believe, that he sees details that I can't explain yet. But I'm paying attention.

Now... Hollywood loves to include obvious and seemingly miraculous gifts when portraying people with autism. That fascination may lead some to automatically wonder what someone's gift is when they meet someone with autism.

Whether or not that's true with any individual, when a person thinks differently and sees the world in unique ways, it makes sense that they can be catalysts for innovation. More likely, even. I believe that being able to see and experience the world in varied ways opens doors and contributes to progress, artful expressions, and enhances human connections.

Hypersensitivity

"If you look at things from other people's perspectives... it makes it easier to think what we can do to help them out."

~ Max Wiznitzer, Pediatric Neurologist,

University Hospital Rainbow Babies & Children's Hospital in Cleveland

We used to have a difficult time going through small passages like a door with a lot of people standing near the entrance or a tight hallway that opened into a large, crowded space. I think it was like leaving a tolerable space and bursting into one that was just too much too fast. Ryan would dig his feet in, squeeze my hand, and try to pull me back to the section we'd came from.

Things like having an enjoyable day at the aquarium are reasons to celebrate.

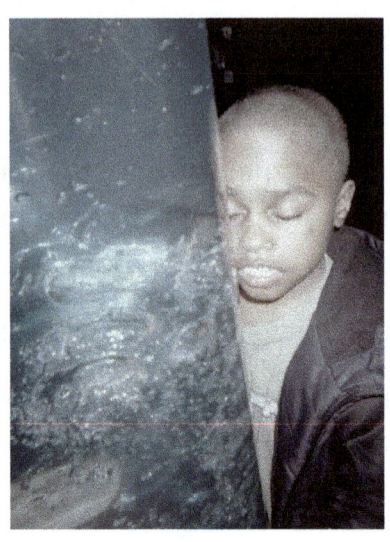

Many with autism are extremely sensitive to things that we may see as typical interactions. Sound, motion, light, and textures may overwhelm them. Some do things to calm themselves like hum, cover their ears, close their eyes, spin, flip their hands, try to drown out overwhelming sounds with sounds of their own, and more. Casual observers often confuse autism-related behavior with misbehavior.

I stumbled on a demo once by game designer, Taylan Kadayifcioglu or Taylan Kay. He was trying to simulate in a video game how it feels to live with hypersensitivity. The demo truly captured feelings of being spatially, audibly, and visually overwhelmed.

Open the Blinds

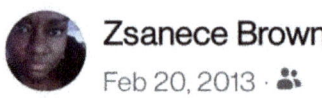

Zsanece Brown
Feb 20, 2013

Whenever I forget to open the blinds and let a little light in, Ry does it for me.

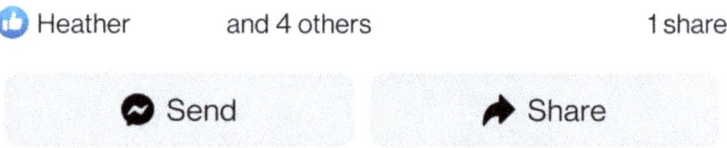

    I didn't learn about joint attention until Ryan showed me what it can be. It's a developmental milestone. It's those moments when a child sees something especially awesome and looks at you with a - *Did you See that?!* - look on their face. Sometimes, pictures of children with autism have captured a "far off" look and some may think that they're disconnected.

    But I've learned to follow Ryan's line of sight. I think the hypersensitivity some have leads to magical moments for them when we think that there's not much to see, hear, or feel.

For example, Ryan has always loved watching the wind's effect on the trees around him. He's drawn my attention to the layered darkness of the bark of a tree. I've sat quietly watching him take in the movement of a plastic bag caught in a gust of wind.

    I started working harder to create moments of joint attention. I follow his line of sight until I'm the one who ends up with a - *Wow, I see it!* - look on my face.

That Dude

My youngest son is affectionate, has an infectious laugh, and is my sometimes shadow. Ryan was "diagnosed" with autism very early, at two years old. Ian was just three and a half years old at the time, still a little dude himself.

We were fortunate enough to have what's called early intervention. For us, early intervention meant exploring a variety of programs that took advantage of learning opportunities during play. An early educator visited our home once a week. We had access to a Tuesday night playgroup that included the whole family. And Ryan went to a half-day class Monday through Friday called Even Start. Think of it as Head Start, but with teaching designed to address developmental delays.

When I dropped Ryan off in the morning, Ian would literally run into the classroom and I'd have to drag my quiet tempest out of there. So, Ian and I developed our own morning routine of daily nature walks, visits to the library, and lunch for just the two of us.

We weren't new to the autism community. I have a nephew who also has autism. I think this contributed to my reaction to Ry's diagnosis and, though I recognized that I didn't know what to expect as far as services needed, I was comfortable with the idea of raising a child with autism.

Why quotes for diagnosed?

    Those who've known me for a while know that I tend to be really quiet at times. So, when Ry's pediatrician made note of how quiet he was during one of his regular check-ups, my first thought was that he may be a lot like me. Ry wasn't just quiet though. He would be so silent that you'd forget that he was in the same room. At the same time, I was dealing with a couple of high stress situations... Quiet in the midst of chaos can be soothing.

    Ry's doctor didn't give me a referral to another medical professional. She gave me the phone number for Child Find which I later found out was part of the Baltimore County Public School System. When the appointment was made, a whole group of people showed up at my house. There was an early educator and therapists with bags of toys. Within minutes, Ry tricked one of them into looking the other way while he grabbed what he wanted. Then, he sat over by the patio window with his back to all of us and played quietly.

The following months involved completing packets of questionnaires that asked for different behavioral and developmental specifics. The initial assessment led to his being placed in Even Start, but here's how the conversation went.

The assessment's results were discussed, and the meeting ended with the question, "So how do you want him classified?"

Now... if you've seen me give the side eye in person, that's exactly what happened next. I was confused. I mean, I thought they were the experts. How could I tell them what the results of all of those assessments meant? Where were my answers?

At the time, I could choose between a designation of autism or one of pervasive developmental delay. Part of their explanation hinted at the idea that some parents don't want their child's designation to be autism. I was close to being irritated at that point because I wasn't there to figure out my personal preferences. I needed to know what I should do next. According to the team, a designation of autism meant that more resources would be available to him... *Really? Well, let's go with autism.*

    Years later when I needed the doctor's office to fill out some paperwork, I was told that there wasn't a medical diagnosis of autism on file for Ryan. The diagnosis on file in his medical records was developmental delay.

    We were given a referral to see the specialists at Kennedy Krieger. Even though Ry had worked with early childhood development specialists through the school system for years, the specialist at Kennedy Krieger is the one who gave him his medical diagnosis of autism to match the designation he's had with the school system since he was two years old.

A slowly exhaled breath

I feel my mistakes...

bold-faced and sans serif,

heavy with inflections.

Our connections are...

perilously straining.

What if I break them,

unable to mend them as I'm

too often uncertain?

I remember my dreams.

And it seems as if their

amendment...

was a redirection.

I reimagined my purpose.

And it was...

within those waking moments

that I would

begin to breathe from my center,

surreptitiously training my thoughts...

removing barriers to greatness.

I believe that my presence

is by design, that I'm drawn

to those with which I am aligned...

that I'm built for more than this

Spontaneous Language

 Zsanece Brown
Mar 2, 2016

Me to FussyPants: If you don't stop that nonsense...
Ry: I need nonsense!

How... how do you respond to that? >.>

    The skills that typically contribute to early language development are a huge part of our current day-to-day lives. Echolalia is the repetition of words or phrases. It's often listed as one of the signs of autism, yet it's also typical in early language development with it fading away as the child begins to use more spontaneous language.

    When I'm talking to Ry, he tends to immediately repeat the last two words. During the day, he may use a lot of repetitive two-word phrases that can seem random and out of context.

But then there was the night-night "argument" we used to have. When I told him night-night, he would immediately repeat the phrase but add "I *not*."

"I *not* night-night."

Ok... you're using language to disagree and adding in some spontaneous language that you understand communicates your displeasure with the situation. Well played, sir. Well played.

Expressive Language

Normally, Ry can be stuck in what I've called a request/response bubble.

"I want cookie, please."

Oftentimes I need to respond with, "Almost" or "Wait, please." After just a few minutes he'll make the same request, and I'll respond as I did before.

I rarely present new or additional information in my subsequent responses because I've recognized how that sometimes creates a separate understanding process. Or it resets a conversation. I've seen this in neuro-typical interactions. We're so accustomed to overstimulation and information saturation that we can tune out nuanced connections.

So when Ryan and I are having the same conversation, I keep the words the same to limit confusion and prevent a reset. This time, he initiated a new conversation while extending the previous one. All on his own.

"I'm mad you."

His growth in understanding and using language is exciting. His expressions are indicative of his personality as much as it is for his neuro-typical peers.

Modeling Language

One of Ryan's challenges has been recognizing that someone is asking him a question and waiting for an answer. He may think that you're "modeling" language, in other words, demonstrating what he can say next. He's learning the difference though.

Expanding expressive language also means that he'll recognize how to tell someone how he feels. I've chosen not to model "I'm ok" or "Fine" as the expected response to "How are you?" Sometimes we're not ok.

I'm fine.

Comfort me with your truth,

your authenticity, your

aversion to hiding your real from me...

Tell me how you're feeling,

without the need to consider

if that appeals to me.

Disregard what we've been taught...

the disingenuous asking,

the tasking

of "fine" responses.

Share what has you reeling,

without the worry of

if that bothers me.

I believe in alchemy. That

moments, once unsettling...

contribute to your artistry.

And I would paint with you,

write of those lingering imprints

and those parts of you

that you no longer need to hide,

those

varied shades of blue,

those distinct and unblended strokes of color,

your tangible means of intensity...

complete and duly framed.

Only then could "I'm fine" be true.

Adapting with Technology

Letting Ry send texts on my phone.
He sent 🍗🍟 to Ian.

👍 Suzanna   and 5 others   10 comments

💬 Send   ➤ Share

    Ryan is of the generation that's connected to technology in ways that my generation wasn't. It's always had some presence in their lives, whereas my childhood included always carrying a quarter for the phone booth as part of my emergency plan. I timed running to the kitchen for snacks so as to get back to a show or movie before the commercial break was over.

    Ryan has always watched how we use our devices. He would pay attention to not just what he saw on the screen but also how we navigated using the apps. He recognized cause and effect. And he was successful in his early attempts to use technology on his own.

On Friday nights, we tend to order in. The boys usually take turns choosing what we eat. Ryan used to point to pictures on a menu to let us know what he wanted. His first text was a request for "chichen" and fries.

Non-verbal Communication

Ryan understands conversations happening around him even though he's not actively participating in them. He may not even be making eye contact, but he has immediate responses to things that we say or do. And his ears always perk up if we're talking about treats. Always.

I'm still caught off guard though by conversations that he responds mischievously to, like the time he heard me tell my mom that I was going to cut his hair later that night. I walked her to the door. When I turned around, I saw that he'd hidden the clippers and returned to where he was sitting with his hands innocently clasped on his lap. That was the funniest "absolutely not" that he'd clearly communicated to date.

Virtual Learning

The year was 2020, the beginning of the global coronavirus pandemic and the early attempts of getting back to normal. Things like Zoom calls, WebEx meetings, and Google Classroom were incorporated into our day-to-day lives. These helped us connect to each other and offered that visual element many need in communication.

Balance was a challenge. There were times when adaptations seemed limited. We used them to fill in gaps, mimicking elements that we were used to. Inasmuch as we did the best that we knew how, opportunities to truly shift how we interact were missed.

I understood what Ryan communicated when he deleted Google Classroom. I just didn't realize that he knew *how* to do that. Of course, it was reinstalled. But we made a point of paying attention differently to his limits regarding engagement and the need to incorporate other sensory needs and meaningful breaks. Some of the compromises included taking the classroom outside, getting on the other side of the camera and taking pictures as part of the lesson, and including the MOs.

How well did the rest of us communicate our changing needs during this time? What are we doing differently now? What have we learned?

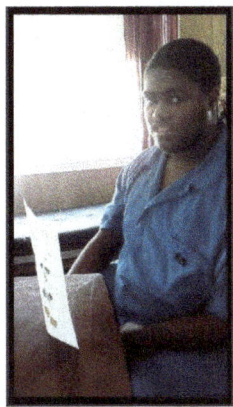

Community-based Instruction

Zsanece Brown
May 3, 2011

Just signed Ry's permission slip for a trip and had him sign on the line that said he will adhere to bcps's rules and regulations. I feel like I'm being deceptive. Plus he laughed after he signed it...

👍 Like   💬 Comment

Van

    Community-based instruction (CBI) is a teaching strategy that helps students with disabilities learn, develop, and practice skills necessary to function in our communities. These focused skills include activities that help individuals live independently.

    Ryan worked hard to earn points that he could redeem in the school store. He often bought cookies with his points. Understanding how exchange worked in a controlled environment in the school store could then be put into practice while out and about in the community. To help make the experience feel even more personalized, his debit card has his picture on it.

Cookies Are Life

Zsanece Brown
Jan 23, 2019

Ry is in my room with me since I'm kinda drowsy. First he gave me a kiss with cookie breath. When I looked away, he reached in his pocket then turned his back to chew. Turned back around with a straight face. 😊

😆 Suzanna   and 7 others

💬 Send   ➤ Share

Zsanece Brown
May 2, 2021

This boy is on Instacart again 😊
My cart has Double Stuff Oreos from Aldi's and he's now browsing Sprouts...

😆👍 Alecia   and 6 others   6 comments

💬 Send   ➤ Share

MOs Are Master Negotiators

I folded immediately.

MOs are also partners in crime...

Zsanece Brown
Mar 6, 2021

So... I was coming upstairs from the basement and I heard someone run out of the kitchen. The fridge was slightly open because a MO was on the floor and keeping it from closing... 🙄

Someone's legal team may come for me, but whatever. I saw what I saw.

💙💚💛🧡

🤣❤️ Suzanna   and 8 others   11 comments

💬 Send   ➤ Share

    The first group of MOs that Ry carried with him everywhere had voice boxes originally. Ry decided to remove the voice boxes and he started using the emptied pockets as storage. For cookies.

    It didn't take long for him to start including the MOs in other capers. Ry's quick. He hears your approach and will dart so as to not be caught doing something he knows he's not supposed to be doing. It usually involves snacks. If a MO is dropped while he's in flight, they've got to fend for themselves.

But here's how my mom folds. It isn't Ry who's caught. It's the MOs. And she'll have a stern talking to whichever MO is left behind while Ry stands there intently listening.

~*~

Ryan is allowed either one MO or two monkeys to take to school with him. Monkeys are little, colorful manipulatives that are used in occupational therapy or in math class. They're primary colors. He loves them. They're small enough for several of them to fit in the palm of his hand.

They're a mixture of animals. There are monkeys, teddy bears, tigers, and more. But we got into the habit of calling the collection of them "monkeys" because those were the first animals in the group that he identified.

During casual conversations I'll usually ask him, "How many do you have? Count them." And he'll say in response, "One. Two" or "One. Two. Three. Four."

But one morning, when he was getting ready for school and where he has a set number of monkeys that he can take with him, my mom asked him to tell her how many monkeys he had. Ryan said, "One. Two. One. Two."

She thought that something was up. She took care of something in the kitchen, then came back... kind of like a reset. She asked him again, "How many monkeys do you have?"

This dude started smiling. He actually had four monkeys. He just said "One. Two" twice.

My mom, (also known as) Ma

I'm a lover of nature and I get consumed in the beauty of the heavenly bodies as well as what our earth provides from season to season. But these same things are seen and enjoyed from a different and unique perspective from a child who has no concept of limit or boundaries or what seems impossible to the common mind of others.

Ryan can take a soft, stuffed toy and have it stand up in the middle of the floor without support or prop. He can balance that same soft toy on the top of a door or a banister. Ryan has also taken a sheet of paper that was an assignment and stand it straight up, without anything in front of it or behind it. I am amazed at how he sees things and what he will accomplish.

I sit, with the camera ready, waiting to capture what Ryan will accomplish next. I learn so much, seeing things through Ryan's eyes.

What will that dude and his MOs do next?

What I think I love more than anything is how Ryan recognizes when he's accomplishing a skill. He'll be so excited to show you what he knows. He's proud of himself. And he'll repeat his understanding, then build on it… in his own time.

I was taught that we retain the most information when we teach someone else. So, when Ryan started "teaching" his MOs things like washing up, getting dressed, and setting the table for dinner, I was so excited that I would hold my breath. I didn't want to miss a thing.

When I do miss these moments, my mom captures them for me. She noticed that Ryan shifted from rote responses to truly connecting through reading. She made a game out of shopping and included him in writing the list. Ryan let her know what he wanted from the store, and she wrote everything down. Then she told him, "Mommy is going to buy it."

So, when I got home, he presented his shopping list to me and said, "I want. Buy it. Cookie, please." He was so incredibly proud of himself as he read the list, pointing at each word.

We framed it.

Scan the QR code to hear how proud he was of himself.

~ * ~

What I look forward to more than anything is what I'll learn next from Ryan... because there are times when I honestly feel a bit rudderless. Sometimes I feel like I'm missing opportunities to make sure that this family is ok.

On the other hand, I've accepted that I'm currently resting. I'm resting as a necessary and physical response to trauma, stress, health scares, loss, and so much more. So, my focus has shifted. And I'm following Ry's lead somewhat.

I'm looking for ways that allow him to express creativity, awareness, and love. I'm waiting to see that realization in his eyes that he's being heard and seen. And I hope that those around us continue to tap in and join us in whatever ways they can.

Special Thanks

Some of the friends and chosen family who offer encouragement and support when we share part of our story or moments that are important:

Danyell	Heather	King	Kim
Kimberly	Suzanna	Leva	Mia
Alecia	Van	Lori	Jarrod

Ryan's "legal team" has grown from the three original partners to a host of associates. Please don't come for him on social media. They respond promptly, tag each other, and they'll bring receipts.

About the Authors

Zsanece Brown is a Creative, author, writer, poet, visual producer, vocal artist, and recording artist.

Born in Baltimore, Maryland in 1976, much of her poetry is inspired by dreams and love, longing, and the comfort found in silence. Her work has often been described as bordering on the metaphysical, finding connections between seemingly dissimilar things.

The first piece that she recognized as a poem was written at 16 years old but like so many other Creatives, writing was how she expressed herself at a very young age. As an avid reader, drafting story ideas came naturally. Later, writing was therapy and for her eyes only.

Once she shared her writing, connection became the purpose. Some would open up to her in response to that connection and often for the first time.

Starlitecafe was the first poetry community that she was a part of for almost 10 years. The daily workshops and weekly writing challenges encouraged collaboration and continue to influence how she connects with other Creatives. Deliberate connection and opportunities to collaborate is why she shares her work.

Graphic design, visual production, sound mixing, and recording is part of how she collaborates. Her current price list compensates for the detailed work and time that goes into visual production, but it's not something that she advertises. Essentially Creative isn't the goal; it supports the goal.

Consetta Brown was born and raised in Baltimore, Maryland. She loves to draw and enjoys calligraphy. She's a lover of nature and gets consumed in the beauty of the heavenly bodies as well as what our earth provides from season to season.

Coming Soon

be·Cause

by Zsanece Brown

Indigo

Jet black

water slapping like ink

spilling on jagged rocks.

Subdued and muffled voices

in the distance,

in clusters...

along the shores of the

darkest blue.

First light highlights

dulled hope on

bright orange vests,

disbursing vast search parties

determined to find you.

Losing you is like

drowning...

slipping into what hollow feels like.

Indigo

voices echoing in layers

throughout the night,

calling you by name -

your first and your last.

Bright lights, white circles

moving and casting beams,

disbursing scurrying witnesses

that cannot speak of you.

Searching for you sounds like

cracking sticks

and the distraction

of crunching leaves.

Royal blue

eyes bouncing from and to

another locked window,

silently check-listing

each closed door,

pausing

and then dissolving

through the one that isn't.

The direction I choose to run in

might take me farther from you.

Losing you feels like…

vomiting violently

and arms that shouldn't be empty.

Sky blue

peeking through our

favorite shades of green.

Barefoot,

lying in grass warmed by the sun.

My son is

so much like me. He

sees the world as is,

but differently.

Knowing you is like

learning in ways I was supposed to

and treading water.

www.ingramcontent.com/pod-product-compliance
Lightning Source LLC
Chambersburg PA
CBHW051659090426
42736CB00013B/2451